THEN & NOW

LEHIGH COUNTY

THEN & NOW

LEHIGH COUNTY

Kelly Ann Butterbaugh

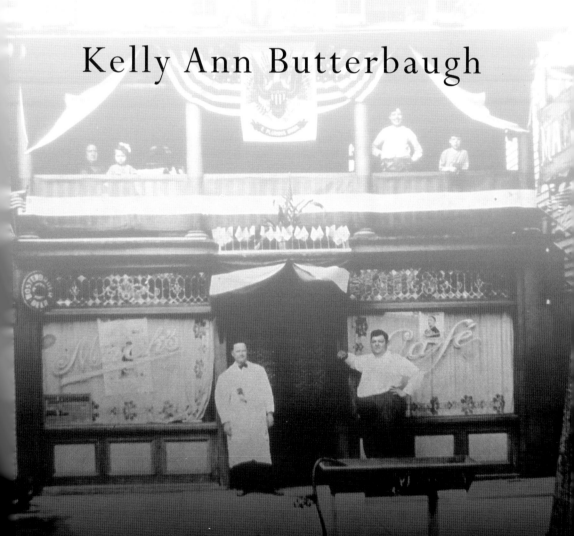

For my family, who is part of this book in so many ways

Library of Congress Control Number: 2010932961

Published by Arcadia Publishing
Charleston, South Carolina

Printed in the United States of America

For all general information, please contact Arcadia Publishing:
Telephone 843-853-2070
Fax 843-853-0044
E-mail sales@arcadiapublishing.com
For customer service and orders:
Toll-Free 1-888-313-2665

Visit us on the Internet at www.arcadiapublishing.com

ON THE FRONT COVER: On the front cover is Mack Trucks' Plant 4 during the mid-1950s. Henry J. Nadig was the first man to build a car in Allentown, and he put it together on this site in 1889. Mack trucks were built in Allentown from 1905 until 1987. In 1989, redevelopers purchased Plant 4 and converted it into the Bridgeworks Industrial Complex. (Courtesy of the Mack Trucks Historical Museum.)

ON THE BACK COVER: The back cover shows the swimming pond at Ontelaunee Park, an amusement park in New Tripoli. (Courtesy of the Lynn-Heidelberg Historical Society.)

Contents

ACKNOWLEDGMENTS

No one person can write a history book. So many people were involved in the creation of this book, and I am forever grateful to them. Thank you to these organizations for donating photographs and information: the Historic Catasauqua Preservation Association, the Coopersburg Historical Society, the Library of Congress Photographic Division, the Lower Milford Historical Society, the Lynn-Heidelberg Historical Society, the Mack Truck Museum, the Macungie Historical Society, the Old Fairground Association of Allentown, Railways to Yesterday, the U.S. Geological Society, the Union United Church of Christ in Neffs, and the Whitehall Historical Preservation Society.

Special thanks go to those who went out of their way to help me. My unending gratitude goes to: Robert Reinbold for providing photographs and an amazing amount of Rittersville research, Robert Metzger for his postcards, Bob Grim for his help with Whitehall research and photographs, Ted Zapach for his photographs and for restoring a great old barn, Evelyn Yost for her photographs and her memories, Linda and Tom Vanim for sharing their family history and photographs with me, Frank Whelan for all his great articles—thanks for preserving history for us, Joseph Yurko for his trolley expertise and for acquiring photographs, Doug Peters for welcoming me into the Railways to Yesterday museum, Bruce Young for his family photographs and genealogy, Bob LeFevre and the members of the Historic Catasauqua Preservation Society for opening their museum to me, Ginny Woodward for her help with research, Tara Henninger for inviting me into the Neffs Memory Room, Janis Wilson of the U.S. Geological Society for her assistance, Pastor Rick Paashaus for donating Mildred Musselman's collection of photographs, Cliff Benner for his images and assistance, Don Schumaker of the Mack Truck Museum for photographs, Stephen Kulik for sharing his family's history and photographs, and Jeff Donat for his help with research.

A special thank you goes to my family, not only for helping me to find the time to do what I love but also for sharing their history with me. I have put something for each one of you in the book. I especially thank my son, Christopher; my grandmother, Mary Kraynek; and my husband, Bob, for helping me take the present-day photographs.

All of the now images in the book were taken by the author, Kelly Ann Butterbaugh. Unless otherwise noted, historical photographs are from the author's personal collection.

INTRODUCTION

Change is a dynamic concept, one that gives and takes. Lehigh County is no stranger to change. It is not a community frozen in time but one that has continued to evolve. In 1895, Lehigh County's population was 93,893. By 2009, the population was 343,519. Less than 30 years ago, the county seat of Allentown rarely appeared on national maps. With a population of 107,294 in 2006, it is now a major city known nationwide. Since its inception on March 6, 1812, Lehigh County has been constantly transforming, and the changes have proven to be successful.

This 347-square-mile county was originally part of Bucks County. It later was taken as part of Northampton County before becoming independent. It bears the name Lehigh, derived from the Native American word *lechauweki*, which means "where the stream forms a fork." This word was then changed by settlers to "lecha" and then later construed into "lehigh." When it was originally part of Northampton County, the area that was the west fork of the Delaware River was called Lehigh, or Lecha.

As the county changed, so did the villages within it. Allentown has always been the largest town. Yet, while it was settled by William Allen in 1735, Allentown was originally named Northampton Town until 1838. It is not uncommon for one village's residents to know two names for their home. What some called South Allentown others called Aineyville, the 19th Ward, Mountainville, or even Smiths.

Industry inspired the names and growth of many of the villages in the county, however, many of those industries no longer exist today. The village of Egypt really did not blossom until 1884 with the advent of the American Cement Works. This caused a boom of 37 homes, a hotel, a railroad, a post office, and a population of 175. The limekilns of Lower Milford Township caused Charleston to be renamed Limeport. Catasauqua was originally known as Craneville when it housed the nationally known Crane Iron Works. To eliminate confusion between it and a New York town of the same name, the new name of Sideropolis was suggested in 1845. No one knows why, but the change never took place, and the town was named after the Catasauqua Creek instead. Interestingly, the town of Hokendauqua was actually built by the Thomas Iron Company. The company established schools, planned streets, and organized a town for its workers around the iron plant. Owner David Thomas suggested the name Hokendauqua from the Delaware word *hokin*, meaning "land," and *dochwe*, meaning "to seek." It was a word the Delaware used to refer to the Irish settlers in 1730 and was more of an exclamation than a name. Hokendauqua was laid out on November 9, 1854, by the Thomas Iron Company, much like Slatington was planned by the Lehigh Slate Company in 1851.

Despite all the debate over the name Hokendauqua, the town originally was going to be named Coplay. Present-day Coplay was named Schreibers before it took the discarded Hokendauqua name upon becoming a borough in 1869. Meanwhile, West Coplay was renamed Stiles because mail consistently went to the wrong town. People started to address their mail to Mr. Stiles, the postmaster, rather than to West Coplay to alleviate the confusion.

Town names continued to change. Another change brought about by postal confusion was Siegersville, better known as Orefield. Just north of the village was another named Saegersville, causing confusion between post offices. Siegersville vacillated between this name and Orefield for decades. Before the cement companies came, the village known as Cementon was better known as Whitehall Station after the train depot there. Coopersburg was not named after Judge Peter Cooper until 1832, before which it was known as Frysburg after Joseph Fry. Fullerton began as Ferndale, until it was developed and named to honor James W. Fuller. Many smaller towns were absorbed by Allentown over time, but they informally retain their names today. Rittersville became the 15th Ward, Mountainville is the 19th Ward, Hilltown is known as the 17th Ward, and Greisemersville mostly falls in the 18th Ward.

Some changes are amusing to those who hear of them today. In a 1914 history, Hokendauqua was described as a town that "contains no place where liquor is sold" in agreement with the Thomas Iron founders' decree. The owners planned to sell land only to those working for the iron company, hoping to exclude negative vices from their town. Yet residents know that in the early part of the 20th century, after Thomas Iron has closed, not one but two beer distributors took residence in the town along Front Street, just below the Thomas Mansion where the superintendent of the iron works lived.

Not so amusing to many is the change from rural to suburban. An 1860 history book states, "We may confidently calculate that in a quarter of a century (or probably only half of that time) the manufacturing interest of the county will largely overbalance the agricultural."

This certainly was an accurate predication, as the county began to welcome industry. Yet the industry gave way to change as well, leaving a county that had been transformed from agriculture to industry with abandoned factories and unemployed workers. Companies that everyone thought would last forever didn't. Silk mills that covered two or three city blocks during operation were abandoned and converted into condominiums. In 1948, when the Lehigh Valley Dairy was heralded by trade magazines as "America's Most Beautiful Dairy," no one expected it to become a demolished pile of bricks by 2011. And finally, no one who looked at the once endless line of Mack trucks awaiting delivery could have imagined that the company would move south and leave behind abandoned, weed-covered fields as a reminder of days gone by.

Eventually, farming and industrial giants were crowded out by retailers, corporations, and housing developments. Today 18,000 acres of farmland and 17,000 acres of parkland are preserved in hope of keeping the rural reminders of Lehigh County alive. Preservationists work toward this end, but as those before us learned, change is unstoppable. When farmers set forth to till their fields for the 1954 season, they never expected the piles of stones and machinery that would soon come with the Pennsylvania Turnpike. Residents in the southern part of the county did not expect to uproot their homes in 1984 to get out of the way of the final stretch of Interstate 78. And how the present would surprise the woman who once berated a young, soon-to-be historian in the 1940s for taking a picture of a trolley car because "it's a waste of film to take a picture of something that'll come by every day."

With all these changes, it is impossible to fit the history of Lehigh County into less than 100 pages. I had to accept that. Instead, it became my responsibility to choose those photographs that best represent the county as it was and as it is now. What changes will come in the next 100 years? No one knows. Change is unsettling sometimes, but it makes room for the future. No one can live in the past, but we can work to preserve it.

CHAPTER 1

MAIN STREETS

Looking west on Hamilton Street from Lumber Street is the old shopping district of Allentown. In 1811, there were only six stores here. The names of Allentown's streets today are not those of the original city plan, though a few remain. Today's names were set in 1853 when the houses received numbers for the first time. Allentown officially became a city on March 12, 1867. In 1902, the town still did not have one paved street.

Many towns in Lehigh County are named after prominent residents while some, like New Tripoli, have more unique origins. Legend says that the town was named in honor of the U.S. Navy's victory over Tripoli during the Barbary Wars in 1816. Before Madison Street, as it is seen here, was settled, many of the county's residents feared Native American attacks. In 1756, the entire Zeisloff family was massacred. Their log cabin was preserved and relocated in 2001 to Ontelaunee Park. (Historical photograph courtesy of Robert Metzger.)

The town of Egypt was named in honor of the country because the soil here seemed equally as fertile to the first settlers. Early records list the town as Egypta. It remained a very small community until the American Cement Works opened in 1884, bringing a boom to the area. In 1913, the town proudly had 15 automobiles. To the right is the Egypt Hotel (now known as Riley's) that Jacob Steckel built in 1790. (Historical photograph courtesy of the Whitehall Historical Preservation Society.)

When the area around today's Race Street in Catasauqua was known as Biery's Port, the west bank of the river was known as the Pennsylvania Shore, and the east bank was known as the Jersey Shore. Along the Jersey side, a covered bridge replaced the original chain bridge in 1852. This covered bridge is the second, having been built in 1862 after the first was destroyed by a flood. Thirty years later, an iron bridge replaced this one beside the *c.* 1835 Biery home. (Historical photograph courtesy of the Historic Catasauqua Preservation Association.)

Originally named Ferndale, Fullerton was renamed around 1865 after James T. Fuller began to plan building lots for the growing community. With a population that nearly quadrupled between 1884 and 1913, Fullerton had always been an industrial area until recently when it turned towards retail businesses. This 1892 view of Third Street shows the changes over time, as the dirt road is now paved and congested with automobiles. (Historical photograph courtesy of the Whitehall Historical Preservation Society and the Fullerton Fire Company.)

Today's Hanover Avenue began in 1876 as the Rittersville Pike, a toll road. By 1915, Allentown widened Rittersville Pike, and residents uprooted houses and pushed them back to allow for the expansion. The new road proved to be still too narrow, as seen by parts of Hanover Avenue today. After closing its post office on June 30, 1899, Rittersville's battle for independence was over on February 16, 1920, as it was annexed by Allentown to become the 15th Ward. (Historical photograph courtesy of Robert Reinbold.)

In 1776, Peter Miller established the village of Millerstown. It became a borough in 1857, and on November 8, 1875, the residents changed the borough's name to Macungie to reflect the original Lenape name for the area. The name translates to "the feeding place of the bears," and when mixed with early Pennsylvania German, it became "bear swamp." Original spellings varied, and early maps call it Macht Kunshi, Machkunschi, and Macongy—among others. Like the town of Vera Cruz, Macungie was once rich in jasper mines. (Historical photograph courtesy of the Macungie Historical Society.)

The Vera Cruz Tavern is the oldest tavern in the county, having been built in 1738. Vera Cruz also includes the oldest jasper mine pits in the country. The Native American paths to the jasper pits evolved into the crossroads at the tavern. Here the main road has been paved and widened over time, losing its tree-lined appearance, but the quaint homes show few changes.

Looking south on Limeport Pike, the corner of one of the original hotels (right) can be seen, with its carriage house on the left. The current owners believe the original two-story section was built in 1753. The town was originally known as Charleston, but the booming lime business brought a new name and three taverns to the small town. During this time of industry, wagons awaiting loads of lime would stretch for nearly a mile down the road. (Historical photograph courtesy of Clifford Benner.)

n St., Looking South, Limeport. Pa.

At the intersection of Main and State Streets in Coopersburg stands the 1829 Eagle House (left), known as the Barron House after David Barron bought it from Peter Cooper in 1868. Later owner Charles Pechacek made the transition from housing teams of horses in the stable to providing gasoline for automobiles, as evidenced by the pumps seen here. Across the street was the original Coopersburg First National Bank (front right) and Wismer's Store (second right), which were both razed. (Historical photograph courtesy of Pastor Rick Paashaus, from the Mildred Musselman collection.)

TRANSPORTATION

Potatoes have continuously been a cash crop in Lehigh County. In February 1918, farmers delivered potatoes to the Hoffman warehouse near the Tripoli Station. This branch of the Reading Railroad was known as the Berksy line. All that remains today of this scene are the potatoes—neither the station nor the Reading Railroad tracks remain. (Historical photograph courtesy of Robert Metzger.)

In 1907, the Lehigh Valley Station in Allentown was heralded as "one of the finest in the state." It sat beside the Allentown Station and the 1837 stone bridge spanning the Jordan Creek. The top of the county prison can be seen in the distant right in both images. Built on pillars along the Jordan River, the station was torn down in 1962. On February 4, 1961, the last passenger train out of the Lehigh Valley left Allentown.

While Route 309 originated as part of the Native American Minsi Trail, this portion connecting Coopersburg to Allentown was built in 1929, three years after the highway was signed into commission. Newspapers heralded the new road as a solution to the harrowing curves and grades of the original route, calling it "one of the meanest stretches of the Old Bethlehem turnpike." The original 3.21-mile stretch was 18 to 20 feet wide and cost $197,790 to build. (Historical photograph courtesy of Pastor Rick Paashaus, from the Mildred Musselman collection.)

The northeast extension of the Pennsylvania Turnpike connects Scranton to Philadelphia. Construction began in 1954 and was completed in 1957, coming through Lehigh County in 1955. A portion of the Yost farm in Lower Milford was lost to a stretch of the highway. The large stone heap was located on valuable farmland. The stone was removed from the highway's cut in the hillside and then crushed on site and used to pave the roadway. (Historical photograph courtesy of Evelyn Yost.)

Trolleys seen inside the Fairview carbarn in 1939 were purchased second hand from the Ohio and the Cincinnati and Lake Erie Railroads. Only a few years old, they were part of the Modernization Program that replaced the original trolleys of the Lehigh Valley Transit Company. The trolley routes were replaced in the early 1950s by bus routes, which mimicked the path of the trolleys. Meanwhile, the trolley barn on Fairview Avenue was converted to a LANTA bus garage. (Historical photograph courtesy of Railways to Yesterday.)

Electrified transportation came to Lehigh County in 1891, but it was not a successful business until Harry Trexler started the Lehigh Valley Transit Company in 1905. In 1925, busses began operating as the Lehigh Valley Transportation Company, but the trolleys continued as the primary source of mass transit. Slowly, trolley lines were converted to bus routes, and finally on June 8, 1953, public busses took over the last of the trolley routes. Lehigh Valley Transit went out of business in 1973. (Historical photograph courtesy of Railways to Yesterday.)

A car from the Liberty Bell route climbs the south side of Lehigh Mountain at Summit Lawn. It is at the base of this incline that the trolley came to a crashing stop on December 23, 1924, only a few days after the start of the route, killing several riders. Today the trolley's path serves as a private access road to homes, and South Pike Avenue roughly follows the trolley route down the mountain.

Here men work to lay trolley tracks near their terminus at what was the Continental Hotel along today's Route 100. Trolley service first extended from Allentown to Emaus in 1898, and the Emaus-Macungie trolley line operated from 1899 until 1929. Many roads in Lower Macungie Township were not named until the 20th century when the county mandated names, thus, the number of roads throughout the county reflect the businesses or residents located on them. (Historical photograph courtesy of the Macungie Historical Society.)

CHAPTER 3

BUSINESSES

In 1900, the Blue Mountain slate quarry near Slatington was one of nearly 100 slate quarries in the Washington Township area. The town of Slatington was originally laid out by the Lehigh Slate Company in 1851. Nearby Slatedale also owes its origins to the industry. Today the Penn Big Bed Slate Company is the only working slate quarry in northern Lehigh. (Historical photograph courtesy of the U.S. Geological Survey.)

Zentner's gas station was located along the grassy strip at the western entrance to the South Mall. The small station faced Lehigh Street at the original Country Club Road intersection—Country Club Road was rerouted during the construction of the mall. In this

c. 1937 photograph, Mildred Ruth Zentner stands in front of her family's business. The business closed in the late 1950s when the family moved out of Salisbury Township. (Historical photograph by Ken Moser; courtesy of Bruce Young.)

Built in 1852, the American Hotel in Catasauqua was one of the finest in the area. Despite its amenities, it was entirely renovated and modernized in 1889 to become the 32-room structure seen here. Built by Solomon Biery, son of Frederick Biery, it fell into disrepair for some time before being converted into the adult living facility that it is today. (Historical photograph courtesy of the Historic Catasauqua Preservation Association.)

Located at the five-point intersection of Second Street, Union Street, and Howertown Road in Catasauqua, the Union Hotel was built by August Richter in 1871. The small hotel could accommodate eight guests. Richter later sold it to Samuel Wint, who then sold it to Benjamin Whitehall, who later sold it to M. Marward. Finally in 1903, William Walker purchased it, and on October 9, 1911, he sold it to Paul J. Ambrose. After changing hands so many times, the hotel was razed. (Historical photograph courtesy of the Historic Catasauqua Preservation Association.)

Originally a 30-bed hospital with only one operating room, Allentown Hospital was built in 1899 for $16,242. At the time, it was on the very edge of the city, with open fields beyond it. The structure was replaced with a modern building in 1952. It continued to operate until January 14, 2000, when the original maternity ward moved to the Cedar Crest Boulevard facility after 100 years of welcoming babies into the world.

The first hospital in Lehigh County was St. Luke's Hospital in Fountain Hill. The original three buildings, which held about 54 beds total, were dedicated on October 25, 1880. Today it houses 606 beds. The only remaining original pavilion is this Coxe Pavilion. It was endowed in 1914 as an obstetrics ward. The pavilions reflected the belief in fresh air and sunshine for healing, appropriate for a town named after its natural mineral springs.

The Homeopathic State Hospital opened on October 3, 1912. Originally, the surrounding rural area aided the homeopathic approach, but both the approach as well as the hospital's name changed over time. A 1912 report of the hospital declared that it should never have been built at this location. At first, access to the water supply and other problems with the site made maintenance crews dislike the building. The hospital closed on December 31, 2010, and its valuable acreage was sold. (Historical photograph courtesy of Robert Reinbold.)

The Hosensack Post Office sat just below the Hosensack train station. This home that included the post office was built by postmaster William Koffel and his wife, Celinda Koffel. He served as postmaster until the post office was closed on April 23, 1954, and residents were thereafter serviced by the Zionsville Post Office. Trains delivered the mail in those days, with first-class mail and newspapers arriving on morning trains and other parcels and mail arriving on afternoon trains. (Historical photograph courtesy of Linda Vanim.)

The Lehigh County prison has occupied the same site on Fifth and Linden Streets in Allentown for nearly 200 years. Originally built in 1813 for $8,420, the first prison was replaced in 1867. The second prison, seen in the historical photograph, was built for $200,222.95 in 1869 and enlarged in 1908. In 1987, inmates filed a lawsuit, claiming that the conditions of the deteriorating prison violated their rights. The new maximum security prison opened in May 1992.

Standing beside Lehigh Street just outside of Emmaus in 1952 are, from left to right, Janet Heimbach, Mamie Florence Zentner, and Arlene Heimbach. Behind them are the buildings that made up Ralston's Flowers. Ralston's Flowers gave way to Hess's South in 1971. By 1975, the department store added a few small stores to its east side to create the South Mall. In 1986, the mall doubled to today's size and added another anchor store, Jamesway. (Historical photograph courtesy of Bruce Young.)

Wilson Shankweiler was a founding partner of well-known Koch Clothing in Allentown and the owner of the Guthsville Hotel, as well as owning the two Shankweiler hotels. The Orefield Hotel, the first of the two, opened in 1926. In 1934, Shankweiler erected the drive-in theater behind the hotel. The theater continues to operate and is the oldest operating drive-in movie theater in America. The hotel was converted to a funeral home in 2010.

The second Shankweiler hotel opened in East Fogelsville at the intersection of Route 22 and Route 100 in the 1930s. Famous for its chicken-and-waffle dinner, it was managed by Willard and Ruth Miller from 1936 until 1955, the time of this photograph. Outliving its sister hotel in Orefield, the Fogelsville Hotel closed on December 28, 1993. It too has been repurposed, and today it serves as a bank on the busy intersection.

Countless young women were employed in mills throughout the county during the days of silk manufacturing. Amandes R. Schuler, Francis Kline, and William F. Stahler established the Vera Cruz Silk Company in 1909. At a later point, it was renamed the Bond Ribbon Mill. In 1988, the Barebo family purchased the mill and put $400,000 into renovations to preserve its interior beams and structure.

Dery's Silk Mill, Catasauqua, Pa.

The Dery Silk Mill in Catasauqua was built in 1897, and an addition nearly the size of the original building was erected in 1899. During its operation, it was one of the more modern silk factories in the county, producing mostly dress silks and succeeding in the international market. After the influx of Japanese raw silk, owner D. George Dery suffered economic failure and was forced out of his opulent mansion. The mill was converted into apartments in 1984.

In 1934, the Lehigh Valley Cooperative farmers spent more than $100,000 remodeling the Post and Sheldon building into a dairy that was heralded as the most beautiful and successful dairy in the nation. Aptly, the dairy sold $12 million worth of milk in 1954 alone. The dairy bar seen here was added in 1948. The entire building was abandoned by the dairy on January 27, 1989. While Olympic Pools occupies the former dairy bar, the building is slated for demolition.

Fritch Brothers and Bogh roller mills in Macungie was founded by D. D. Fritch, N. D. Fritch, and H. F. Bogh. These men also donated the land for the construction of the Grace Lutheran Church in the late 1890s. In the cooper shop, the mill was making its own wooden barrels using metal hoops that were delivered by train in 1894. Today it is Automotive Service Solutions, a car repair service center. (Historical photograph courtesy of the Macungie Historical Society.)

Located at 202 East Main Street in Macungie, the Singmaster tannery began operating around 1785. It was functional into the late 1890s, when tanneries saw a decline. At that time, its steam power was converted to operate the new creamery on the same site. The creamery shut down in 1918. From there, various buildings were erected, the last being today's Bear Swamp Diner, which, along with others, sits on the original property. (Historical photograph courtesy of the Macungie Historical Society.)

Mack Truck's Plant 4 is in full operation here in January 1925. In 2005, a centennial parade marched through the plant, though it no longer manufactured the vehicles. On September 3, 2009, Mack's corporate headquarters relocated to North Carolina, removing the large fiberglass bulldog from the building on August 12, 2010. The Lower Macungie plant is still in operation, as is the Engineering Development and Test Center on Lehigh Street, which is to become a customer center and museum. (Historical photograph courtesy of the Mack Trucks Historical Museum.)

The Farmers National Bank of New Tripoli was organized in August 1909 and opened its doors as the New Tripoli National Bank on March 1, 1910. It operated until 1968, when a modern building was erected across the street. Today it houses the Lynn-Heidelberg Historical Society and retains its original teller fittings and the look of an early-20th-century bank. The second story was added over time, and the iron doors still stand. (Historical photograph courtesy of the Lynn-Heidelberg Historical Society.)

New Tripoli National Bank, New Tripoli, Pa.

William Drauss built the New Tripoli Hotel in 1887. He later sold it to Menno O. Bachman in 1905, the time of this photograph. Bachman also served as a director of the New Tripoli National Bank. The corner of Decatur and Madison Streets is flanked by two hotels, this one and the Hotel German. Jonas German operated the Hotel German, and later his son-in-law James A. Miller oversaw the rebuilt Miller's Hotel after the original Hotel German burned in 1914. (Historical photograph courtesy of the Lynn-Heidelberg Historical Society.)

Joseph Rauch built a large carriage factory in 1875 in the village originally named Holbensville, which was renamed Pleasant Corner around 1857. Several of his family members worked here, including his sons William and Victor and his son-in-law Amandes Handwerk. Note the carriages poised on the second-story balcony. The factory was still making carriages and wagons in 1920 on the lot located across from the present Heidelberg Township building. (Historical photograph courtesy of the Lynn-Heidelberg Historical Society.)

Leather Corner Post is both a village and a hotel. The hotel originated before the Revolutionary War with owner Ludwig Smith, while John P. Bear erected this building in 1861. Its name attracts the most attention, carrying with it the story of a tannery's stolen leather hide later returned by its guilty thief to the top of a corner hitching post in town. One 1830 map lists the area as Woodrings before the story of the stolen hide originated. (Historical photograph courtesy of Robert Metzger.)

The Coopersburg Granite Works quarried, cut, and polished granite on the east end of Coopersburg along Keewayden Street for more than two generations. The Riu brothers—Marshall, Victor, and Emil—began the business in 1923 using extremely hard granite quarried just outside of town. Victor was a noted granite sculptor with pieces on display in Philadelphia and Washington, D.C. Lloyd Riu, Emil's son, managed the company until his retirement in 1985. (Historical photograph courtesy of Pastor Rick Paashaus, from the Mildred Musselman collection.)

After a raging fire in 1905 destroyed six homes, Rittersville felt the strong need for a fire company. With the support of Dr. Robert Klotz, a fire company was organized on December 18, 1905. It was housed in several locations before this modern building was erected in 1913. It was used until 1953 when the East Side Fire Station replaced it. Today it functions as a social organization and houses four bowling allies and community bingo events. (Historical photograph courtesy of Robert Reinbold.)

Another Singmaster building in today's Macungie is best known as Salvatore's Pizzeria. James Singmaster originally built it as office space in 1889. R. J. Ritter Furniture and Housefurnishing Goods christened the first- and second-floor space while the third floor was reserved for social events. Today the pizzeria occupies the first floor while the second and third floors are apartments. It retains the ornate mansard roof and widow's walk representative of its original time period. (Historical photograph courtesy of the Macungie Historical Society.)

The Dent Hardware Company operated in Fullerton from 1894 until the 1970s. It was the world's largest producer of refrigerator hardware, but it was most noted for its cast iron toys made between 1898 and 1937. Henry Dent began the company and later sold it to the Newhard family, who had been partners with him. Henry T. Newhard served as the fourth president of the company until 1975 when it was sold and used as a textile machinery dealership. (Historical photograph courtesy of the Whitehall Historical Preservation Society.)

The Reliance cement mill, erected in 1905 and later known as Essroc, was the last mill in Egypt built by the American Cement Company of Pennsylvania. Altogether the company had seven operating mills near Egypt, with the first built in 1884. Shortly after Reliance was erected, the cement plants closed and their quarries flooded. The quarry beside Reliance became the members-only Ranger Lake Rod and Gun Club. The ruins of the Reliance mill sit beside the fishing grounds. (Historical photograph courtesy of the Whitehall Historical Preservation Society.)

From 1892 until 1926, the F. G. Kurtz and Company furniture factory in Fullerton employed 120 people on average. Franklin Kurtz, along with George Henn and Walter Schaadt, founded the company. At the time of its establishment, Kurtz, the son of a foundry worker, was only 25 years old. The building burned on August 9, 1988, and new homes were constructed on the newly emptied lot. (Historical photograph courtesy of the Whitehall Historical Preservation Society.)

The Phoenix Silk Company opened Adelaide Mill in 1880. Adelaide Mill sparked the interest and economic success of silk mills throughout Allentown and the county. By 1886, the town was an established silk center, and at one time it was known as the largest in the state. Adelaide Mill turned towards manufacturing synthetic fabrics after World War II and operated as Phoenix Mills until its closing.

Originally, a log tavern stood along King's Road, now Hanover Avenue. By 1850, Michael Ritter had replaced the log tavern with the Rittersville Hotel. In the 1890s, the trolley companies took ownership of it until the February 1896 fire that destroyed the building. The fire was said to have been started by the owner's pet monkey. It was soon replaced with the Manhattan Hotel, seen here in 1905, which was a favorite stop until it was razed in 1922. (Historical photograph courtesy of Robert Reinbold.)

The rural life of Lehigh County can still be seen in Stines Corner, Lynn Township. In the 1940s, the Allentown newspaper, *The Call*, nicknamed the village Lehigh County's unofficial icebox due to its consistently low winter temperature recordings. The village was anchored by the Stines Corner Hotel, which was owned by Russell and Violet Bittner from 1958 until 1969. They sold it to Aileen and Robert McKenney, who operated the hotel up to its conversion into a day care by their daughter. (Historical photograph courtesy of Robert Metzger.)

STINES CORNER, PA. E. G. WIESNER'S HOTEL AND STORE

Asbury Graphite Mill operated for 105 years on Sand Island, a point of Lehigh County that juts into Northampton County. Charles Pettinos's family opened the mill in 1891, never employing more than 30 workers at a time. In 1962, it was sold and operated as part of the Asbury Mills. In March 1996, it was closed and later razed after being labeled an obstacle for Bethlehem's plans to renovate Sand Island. (Historical photograph courtesy of the Library of Congress, Prints and Photographs Division.)

CHAPTER 4

FUN TIMES

While working at the Phoenix clothing factory may not have been all fun and games, the holidays brought a little excitement to the job. As seen here, the women working in the former Adelaide silk mill prepare for their annual Christmas party. Mary Kraynek is seated in the front right of the photograph. The company's slogan at this time was "Always a little better."

In 1883, Reuben Troxell leased his 27-acre property along the Little Lehigh Creek to the state of Pennsylvania as a trout hatchery. John P. Creveling served as the superintendent of the hatchery when this photograph was taken in the 1890s. Today the hatchery operates as part of the Pennsylvania Fish Commission's Cooperative Nursery Program, and visitors walk along the pools feeding the fish, just as they have for generations.

The YMCA building south of center square on Seventh Street in Allentown was dedicated on May 24, 1903. Here boys enjoyed the second-floor swimming pool and other activities. The YWCA had a separate location in town until the present building was completed in 1963 and welcomed both men and women to join. The first floor of this older facility was a produce market during the 1950s.

Dorney Park opened as an amusement park in 1884 after enjoying moderate success as a picnic and fishing grounds. In 1889, it began to see financial success when the Toonerville line, an extension of the Allentown-Kutztown Traction Company trolley, was installed. The trolley ran from the south corner of Allentown Center City to Kutztown and brought visitors to the amusement park along Cedar Creek. This early photograph shows the park when it was known as The Natural Spot.

Seen here in the 1940s is the familiar stone water fountain found near the wooden roller coaster at Dorney Park. The location looks very different today, but it offers the same type of refreshments. The wooden coaster also remains, unlike the stone fountain, which disappeared sometime in the late 1980s when the park underwent massive renovations. Nearby was the original dark ride to the park, the Mill Chute, which was later named Journey to the Center of the Earth.

The Skyclone roller coaster at Central Park operated from 1927 until it burned down in 1935. Riders would get out and push the coaster up the hill on the first few runs of the day before the rails warmed up. Plagued by fires, the decline of the trolleys, and the rise of Dorney Park, Central Park went out of business in 1951. This new housing development sits on the hillside that once held the locally famous coaster. (Historical photograph courtesy of Robert Reinbold.)

The Allentown and Bethlehem Rapid Transit Company opened Central Park in Rittersville on July 2, 1892. The park was filled with rides, picnic grounds, and a menagerie that drew families onto the trolleys and into the park. By 1905, the park had grown to such a success that John Philip Sousa played in its theater and $75,000 worth of rides filled its hillside. After it closed, the area was developed by car dealerships and retail stores. (Historical photograph courtesy of Robert Reinbold.)

In 1910, the Dodson farm near Rittersville was purchased to build a nine-hole golf course and a clubhouse. The Lehigh Country Club opened on April 18, 1912, with its large $32,000 Italian clubhouse garnering the most attention. In 1928, the club gave into the pressure of building an 18-hole course. The clubhouse burned on December 23, 1933, and the location was converted into a shopping center in 1961.

Once a racetrack that hosted cart races, the Allentown Fairgrounds still retains its original grandstand built in 1911. The first fair was held in 1852 on a small plot of land between Union and Walnut Streets. The next year it moved north of Liberty Street. By 1888, the event outgrew the grounds, and it moved to today's fairgrounds. Cancelled only in 1862, 1917, and 1918 due to war, the tradition of the fair is more than 150 years old.

From May 1917 until April 1919, the Allentown Fairgrounds was known as Camp Crane. The camp began as a training facility for the United States Army Ambulance Service but turned its focus to the detection of influenza. The camp was intended for 2,000 men but reached a high of nearly 10,000 soldiers. Showers for the men, 200 at a time, were constructed in what was once the cow barns for the fairgrounds, and the grandstand served as a mess hall. (Historical photograph courtesy of the Library of Congress, Prints and Photographs Division.)

Young Daniel Diefenderfer visits Ontelaunee Park when it was still one of three amusement parks in the county. The park was built in 1929 by Homer Snyder and Mark Hoffman. Lou and Shorty Long then took ownership of it in 1965. Although many country music stars visited its stage, it never became the attraction they had planned. In 1982, the Longs sold it to John Kospiah, who auctioned off the fixtures and rides, including the Ferris wheel, in 1987.

Kulik's pond in eastern Salisbury Township once attracted quite a crowd for ice skating and swimming. The pond sits behind today's Allentown Chiropractic Center on private property that has remained in the Kulik family. Salisbury Township was once double its current size, but annexations by Allentown and the formation of the Fountain Hill Borough chopped it into a small, disconnected town. (Historical photograph courtesy of Stephen Kulik.)

CHAPTER 5

RIVERS AND FARMS

The Crane Iron Company built a covered bridge in 1845 for easy delivery of supplies to its iron furnaces in Catasauqua. After the 1862 flood destroyed it, this replacement was erected. In 1904, the bridge was replaced with a heavier railroad bridge that could handle the larger-style railroad cars then in use by the Catasauqua and Fogelsville Railroad. (Historical photograph courtesy of the Whitehall Historical Preservation Society.

In 1941, government engineers declared the Hamilton Street Dam to be one of the most important structures along the Lehigh canal. The first Allentown bridge over the Lehigh River was a 530-foot chain bridge built in 1814. A wooden bridge followed, but the devastating 1841 flood destroyed it, causing this arch one to be built. The dam also was damaged by floods and repaired by the Lehigh Coal and Navigation Company in 1931 and again in 1942.

The Thomas Iron Company in Hokendauqua was at one time the largest and most productive pig iron company in the country. The company was responsible for founding the town of Hokendauqua, as well as controlling the Ironton Railroad in conjunction with the Crane Iron Company. The company was at its operational peak in this March 13, 1915, photograph. Only the overgrown ruins of a few frame buildings and a carbarn line the Lehigh River today. (Historical photograph courtesy of the Whitehall Historical Preservation Society.)

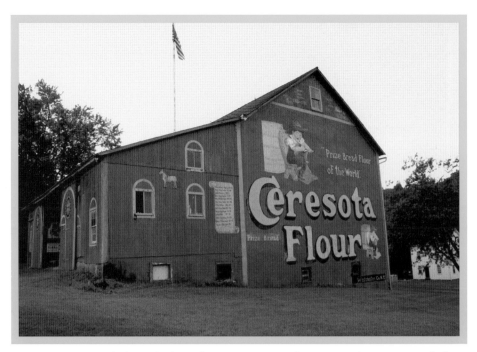

With property records dating back to Thomas Maybury in 1742, Ted Zapach's barn has quite a history. When the famous Mail Pouch Tobacco advertisement on the side of his barn started to fade, Zapach noticed the face of the Ceresota Flour boy peaking through. In 2005, he hired a sign painter to restore the Ceresota advertisement to the barn. Mail Pouch signs were painted on barns from 1890 through 1969, and owners received a yearly stipend for the advertising. (Historical photograph courtesy of Ted Zapach.)

Zapach's Mill off Limeport Pike has been modernized throughout its long history. The earliest documentation of the structure is January 1, 1770, but an enlargement to the mill is reflected in its date stone of 1819. At one point, the side wall of the mill was removed and the stones were replaced after the 18-foot-tall waterwheel was moved inside for use during the winter months. Today the mill and its mechanics are in superior condition. (Historical photograph courtesy of Ted Zapach.)

ARTIFICIAL LAKE
NEW TRIPOLI, PA.

Entrepreneurs once harnessed natural springs and built man-made lakes as they entered the ice business. Harvesting ice in the winter and then packing it inside icehouses, the men would deliver it to homes during the summer months. As the lakes were polluted and refrigeration gained popularity, business slowed.

This man-made lake in New Tripoli was left to grow into a field after the ice business ended. During the summer months, these ice dam lakes were popular places for entertainment. (Historical photograph courtesy of Robert Metzger.)

What was the Duck Farm Hotel in 1814 is now apartments in the section of Allentown once known as Greisemersville. Beside the hotel was Oliver Gittnet's 7-acre duck farm. Visitors paid admission to see the 18,000 ducks, which were raised in pens, though the owner claimed that the visitors upset the ducks so much that he actually lost money when they visited. Those who stayed at Alfred Greisemer's hotel enjoyed a duck dinner each evening of their stay.

The farms surrounding Rittersville disappeared after Dr. Robert Klotz purchased land and gave it away to people who promised to build homes on the land. One of these lots was the Texter farm between East Cedar Street, Hanover Avenue, Oswego Street, and Kearney Street, just behind the Manhattan Hotel. Klotz named the area Park Place and developed it from farmland into a suburban community. He also established his first silk loom mill on the farmland in 1906. (Historical photograph courtesy of Robert Reinbold.)

SCHOOLS AND CHURCHES

Children in Germansville attended this school from 1887 until 1951. At that time, the Lynn-Heidelberg Consolidated School opened, offering schooling through eighth grade. There was no need for small elementary schools like this one anymore. Students who wanted an education beyond eighth grade rode the train into Slatington to attend high school. This photograph was taken in September 1913. (Historical photograph courtesy of Robert Metzger.)

Since 1868, a school has always stood on the corner of Main and Second Streets in Slatington. The first was erected in 1868. The last Slatington high school was built in 1916 and became a middle school once a new high school was constructed in 1959 across town. The district sold the building in 1982, leaving it vacant until the roof partially collapsed on August 1, 2000, and the structure was razed that same year. Only the original flagpole remains.

Of the 17, one-room schoolhouses built in North Whitehall Township after 1843, the Siegersville School was the only one not made of brick. Built of cement block, the school closed less than 10 years after this 1910 photograph was taken. The town of Siegersville changed its name to Orefield in 1830 to eliminate the confusion that the mail service had between it and its northern neighbor, Saegersville. It vacillated between Siegersville and Orefield throughout its history.

Hokendauqua established its school district on April 7, 1865. Like most of the town, the schools were built by Thomas Iron Company. The Hokendauqua High School opened as a two-year high school in 1904, became a four-year high school in 1921, and housed grades 7 through 12 by 1948. In 1911, the Hokendauqua schools became part of the Whitehall Township School District. In 1959, the high school students were moved to the present-day location in Mickleys. (Historical photograph courtesy of the Whitehall Historical Preservation Society.

SCHOOLS AND CHURCHES

After two years of construction, the Fullerton School was dedicated on March 2, 1908. In 1966, the state-mandated redistrict plans forced Whitehall schools to merge with Coplay schools to create today's Whitehall-Coplay School District. The Fullerton School then operated as an elementary school until today's George D. Steckel Elementary School opened in April 1975, closing the schools in Fullerton, Egypt, West Catasauqua, Hokendauqua, and Cementon. The building at Third and Quarry Streets was then renovated into office space. (Historical photograph courtesy of the Whitehall Historical Preservation Society.)

On November 17, 1856, a group of Macungie residents opened the Macungie Institute as a private school in town, with some of its first students from the prominent Singmaster family. Within four years, the school's finances were low enough to suspend classes, and by 1862, it was sold to the town's school district. It served as a public school for the next 127 years, but in June 1989, the school closed its doors to pupils. It was reclaimed as a community center on May 18, 2002. (Historical photograph courtesy of the Macungie Historical Society.)

Allentown's school system began in 1824, but the first high school was established in 1858. That first class of Allentown High School held 14 students, with three graduating. This building on Chew and Lumber Streets was the second Allentown high school. Built in 1880, it served as the high school until 1916 when William Allen High School was constructed. The old Central high school building became an elementary school until the students outgrew it and the new Central Elementary was constructed.

The Mosser School was built in 1917 and still serves the Allentown School District as an elementary school. Named after James K. Mosser, the school is unique in that a separate auditorium, cafeteria, and gymnasium were added to the elementary school in 1969—something no other Allentown school had. The school once housed kindergarten through eighth grade. Today the Allentown School District is the fourth largest in the state and educates more than 18,000 students.

SCHOOLS AND CHURCHES

Cedar Crest College began as the Allentown Young Ladies Seminary on November 3, 1869, at this former retreat known as Clover Nook. Once the college was renamed and moved, this building at Turner and Fourth Streets became the famous College Hotel that hosted celebrities such as Eddie Cantor and Al Jolson. The business declined after a fire destroyed the second floor on January 26, 1939. It closed and was razed in 1964 to be replaced by a parking lot two years later.

Students of Muhlenberg College first met at Trout Hall in Allentown before moving to the present campus in 1904. When the college relocated, it took the new name Muhlenberg College in honor of Henry Melchoir Muhlenberg. At that time it was an all-men's college, becoming coed in 1957. The familiar dome of the old library building (right), now the Haas College Center, is missing in the historical photograph since it was not completed until 1929.

In 1842, Thomas Ritter sold $30 worth of land to Rittersville residents for the first church in town. The church held both Lutheran and Reformed congregations until 1913 when they split. The Reformed congregation built a new church at the same location and renamed it Saint Peter's United Church of Christ, seen here. The influential Dr. Robert and Elizabeth Klotz donated the bell and the altar to the church at its completion in 1914. (Historical photograph courtesy of Robert Reinbold.)

Like many small towns in the county, Alburtis maintained a level of industry that included a silk mill, a mine, and the neighboring Lockridge Iron Furnace. The members of this congregation of the Zion's Lehigh Lutheran Church in Alburtis first met in various homes during 1745. By 1749, land to erect a church was purchased, and the first church was built in 1750. The church building that still stands today was constructed in 1894.

Schools and Churches

Today's Union United Church of Christ in Neffs was built in 1872 on the site of an older stone structure known as the Scrub Oak Church. Seen here in 1955, the church's impressive 165-foot spire can be seen around the region. Beneath the spire is a nearly 2,000-pound bell. In its earliest days, the church built three schoolhouses—one serving as the sexton's house beside the church until 2003, when it was dismantled to allow for an addition. (Historical photograph courtesy of the Union United Church of Christ in Neffs.)

Services before 1924 at the Weisenberg Lutheran Church were spoken entirely in German. Adding English services was one of several changes made since the church's construction in 1864. The second floor was added in 1928, and an addition was built in 1996. This photograph was taken in 1951, five years before the stained-glass windows were added. Today's congregation is a united Lutheran congregation, though it was founded in 1749 as a Union Church with separate Lutheran and Reformed congregations. (Historical photograph courtesy of Robert Metzger.)

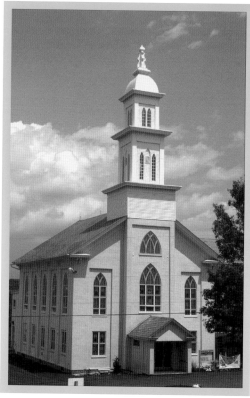

SCHOOLS AND CHURCHES

Today's Ebenezer Church is the third church to stand on the property along Decatur Road. At the time, a Ladies Aide Association formed to help fund the 1824 build. For many years, the ladies group was allowed to meet in the Hotel German for free, and the owners donated supplies for fund-raising ventures. The group's fund-raising paid to install steam heat in 1899 and carpet in 1900. Most importantly, they helped to pay off the church's mortgage. (Historical photograph courtesy of Robert Metzger.)